●Fun with English●

Proverbs

George Beal
Illustrated by Peter Stevenson

Chambers

General editor: John Grisewood
Editor: Nicola Barber
Illustrations: Peter Stevenson
  (Kathy Jakeman Illustration)
Design: Robert Wheeler Associates

CHAMBERS
An imprint of Larousse plc
Elsley House, 24–30 Great Titchfield Street,
London W1P 7AD

This edition published by Chambers 1995
10 9 8 7 6 5 4 3 2 1

A CIP catalogue record for this book is available
from the British Library

ISBN 0 550 325050

Printed in Spain

Proverbs are short, pithy sayings that contain some wisdom or observation on life and people. Many are familiar, such as *He who hesitates is lost* or *A rolling stone gathers no moss*. Some sound profound, but beware of always believing the wisdom of a proverb. Proverbs are not always right or true! Many proverbs contradict others: *Too many cooks spoil the broth* sounds a sensible statement, and so does *Many hands make light work*, yet they each put forward an opposing idea. So you should always be cautious when using proverbs in speaking or writing.

absence
Absence makes the heart grow fonder. You feel friendlier to your friends when away from them.

accidents
Accidents will happen in the best regulated families. Accidents happen to everyone.

accuse
He who excuses himself accuses himself. Anyone who makes a lot of excuses probably knows that they are in the wrong.

accused
Don't ask for pardon before you're accused. Wait till someone says you're guilty before you make excuses.

accuser
A guilty conscience needs no accuser. If you believe yourself guilty, you have accused yourself.

acorn
Great oaks from little acorns grow. Small or humble origins don't mean that you can't reach the top.
Every oak has been an acorn. Things which start small can become large and important.

adversity
Adversity makes a man wise, not rich. Misfortune may not lead to riches, but it teaches you good lessons.
Prosperity makes friends, adversity tries them. Those who stay friends with you when you're poor are your real friends.
Sweet are the uses of adversity. Misfortune is often a blessing in disguise.

advice
Advice when most needed is least heeded. People who need advice are often the most likely to scorn it.
If you seek advice, ask an old man. Those with experience are likely to have greater wisdom.
Nothing is so freely given as advice. People who do not seek advice themselves, are often the first to offer it.

affairs
There is a tide in the affairs of men. A golden opportunity will probably present itself only once.

affection
Affection blinds reason. Love often leads people to do foolish things.

after
After a storm comes a calm. When things are bad you can nevertheless look forward to better times.
After dinner sit awhile; after supper walk a mile. Rest after a heavy meal, take exercise after a light one.

3

AN APPLE A DAY KEEPS THE DOCTOR AWAY!

age
The golden age was the never present age. People always look to the past for the best times. The present day is never ideal.

agree
Birds in their little nests agree. A happy home is one where there is harmony.

all
All's well that ends well. It's the final outcome that matters, despite what happens on the way.
All good things come to an end. No pleasures go on for ever.
All in the day's work. Good and bad, whatever happens is part of life.
All things are difficult before they're easy. However hard a problem appears to be, perseverance will bring its reward.

alone
He travels fastest who travels alone. An ambitious person is more likely to succeed when unencumbered by others.

angels
Fools rush in where angels fear to tread. Foolish people act hastily, while wise people think before they act.

angry
When angry, count to a hundred. After counting to a hundred, your anger will have gone!

answer
A soft answer turneth away wrath. If someone is angry with you, don't show anger in return.

anything
If anything can go wrong, it will. Never assume that nothing will go wrong.

appearances
Appearances are deceptive. Never judge by appearances.

apple
An apple a day keeps the doctor away. Eating healthy food will keep you in good health.
The apple never falls far from the tree. Members of the same family are likely to retain family characteristics.
The apples on the far side of the wall are sweetest. Things which are difficult to get are always the most sought after.
The rotten apple injures its neighbours. A bad thing or person will affect those around it.

army
An army marches on its stomach. A well-fed soldier is likely to be the best fighter.

art
Art is long, life is short (Ars longa, vita brevis). 1. There is so much to learn in life, but only a short time in which to learn it. 2. Art lasts longer than the artist who created it.

ask
Ask no questions and you'll hear no lies. Don't show curiosity.

ass

Every ass likes to hear himself bray.
Fools like the sound of their own
voices.

attack

Attack is the best form of defence. It is
better to take the initiative than to wait
for something to happen.

B

baby

*Don't throw out the baby with the bath-
water.* In an effort to achieve your aim,
don't overlook important details on the
way.

back

His back is broad enough to bear blame.
Describes a person who is strong
enough to bear responsibility.
*You scratch my back and I'll scratch
yours.* Help me out and I'll help you.

bad

A bad penny always comes back. Bad
things always turn up again.
A bad workman always blames his tools.
Describes a person who does a bad job,
and blames everything but himself.

bake

As you bake, so shall you brew. This has
a similar meaning to *As you make your
bed, so shall you lie on it.*

bargain

A bargain's a bargain. You should stick
by your agreements, no matter how
things turn out.
Make the best of a bad bargain. If things
go wrong and you can't change them,
it's best to accept the situation.

barking

Barking dogs seldom bite. People who
make the most noise are usually the
ones who act least.

battle

The first blow is half the battle.
The person who gets in first has the
advantage.

be

Be what you would seem to be. Don't be
a hypocrite.

bear

Bear and forbear. Be patient and
tolerant.

beast

*When the wind is in the east, 'tis neither
good for man nor beast.* Weather
proverb: the east wind is generally a
cold wind.

beat

If you can't beat them, join them.
If what you suggest is totally opposed,
join the majority.

5

beauty

Beauty is but skin-deep. You can't judge things by their appearance alone.
Beauty is in the eye of the beholder. Judging appearance is up to the individual.
A thing of beauty is a joy for ever. Experience of something beautiful remains with you always.

bed

Go to bed with the lamb and rise with the lark. Early to bed and early to rise.
As you make your bed, so you must lie on it. You must accept the consequences of your own actions.

beggar

Set a beggar on horseback and he'll ride to the devil. Someone unused to riches may go badly wrong if wealth suddenly comes their way.

begin

It's good to begin well, but better to end well. Start a job well, but make sure that you see it through to the end.

beginning

Every beginning is hard. Starting something is always difficult.
Everything must have a beginning. Everyone has to start somewhere.

beginnings

From small beginnings come great things. Even the most important things start in a small way.

begins

He who begins many things, finishes but few. If you take on too many different jobs, you won't have time for them all.

believe

Believe not all that you see nor half what you hear. Nothing is ever quite what it seems.
We soon believe what we desire. Most people believe what they want to believe.

believing

Seeing is believing. You are likely to believe what you see with your own eyes.

bend

Better bend than break. Better to wait and consider, rather than be totally opposed to something.

best

The best of men are men at best. However admirable people may be, they are still only human.
The best things come in small packages. Things don't have to be large to be good.
The best things in life are free. This is a line from a popular song, written in 1927.

bigger

The bigger they are, the harder they fall. The more powerful and successful people are, the more they have to lose.

bird

A bird in hand is worth two in the bush. Hold on to what you have, rather than waiting for something better.
The early bird catches the worm. Act quickly and in good time.

Birds of a feather flock together. People are likely to be happier in the company of those with like minds.

bite

If you can't bite, never show your teeth. Don't start trouble if you can't defend yourself.

biter

The biter is sometimes bit. The tables are sometimes turned so that the attacker becomes the victim.

bitten

Once bitten, twice shy. A bad experience makes you want to avoid a second one.

blarney

Kiss the Blarney Stone. Anyone who kisses the Blarney Stone near Cork, Ireland, is said to have the ability to persuade or charm.

blind

If the blind lead the blind, both shall fall into the ditch. Those without knowledge should not try to lead or teach others. *In the country of the blind, the one-eyed man is king.* When people around you are ignorant, even a little knowledge will give you an advantage. *None so blind as those that won't see.* It's pointless trying to convince someone who is totally prejudiced.

blood

You can't get blood out of a stone. You can't get something from someone too mean to give it.

books

Books and friends should be few but good. If you have too many of each, you will have little time to enjoy them.

borrower

Neither a borrower nor a lender be. Borrowing and lending money or possessions can lead to trouble between friends; so it is better not to do either.

borrowing

He that goes a-borrowing goes a-sorrowing. Anything borrowed, especially money, has to be paid back, and the sorrow comes when there's no money left to pay the debt.

bough

Don't cut off the bough you're standing on. Don't get rid of your only support.

branch

The highest branch is not the safest roost. Those at the top have the farthest to fall.

brass

Where there's muck there's brass (or luck). Dirty work can be the most rewarding.

THE BITER BIT.

bread
Bread is the staff of life. You cannot exist without food.

breakfast
If you sing before breakfast, you'll cry before night. Happiness never lasts long.

brevity
Brevity is the soul of wit. A short answer is often the most eloquent.

broth
Too many cooks spoil the broth. Something can be ruined if too many people try to do the same job at the same time.

bull
Take the bull by the horns. Cope with a problem without fear.

bully
A bully is always a coward. Bullies always choose victims among those smaller or weaker than themselves.

burn
Burn not your house to fright the mouse away. Don't go to extremes to solve a simple problem.

butterfly
Break a butterfly on a wheel. Don't use more force than is really needed.

bygones
Let bygones be bygones. Forget past quarrels and forgive.

cake
You can't have your cake and eat it. You must make a decision and stick to it.

candle
Light not a candle to the sun. Don't try to describe the obvious.

cap
If the cap fits, wear it. If the description applies to you, accept it and be warned.

care
Care will kill a cat. Worrying won't help a problem.
'Don't care' was made to care. Those who are careless will discover the folly of their ways.

I'M NOT TAKING THE BULL BY THE HORNS.

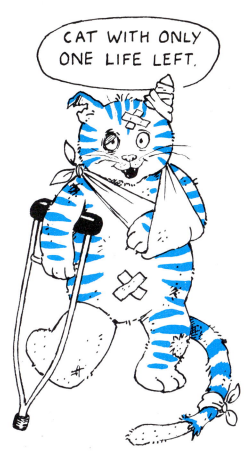

CAT WITH ONLY ONE LIFE LEFT.

cat

A cat has nine lives. A cat seems to escape danger more than other animals.

Like a cat on hot bricks. Describes a worried and nervous person.

When the cat's away, the mice will play. When the person in charge is absent, people will do as they please.

There are more ways of killing a cat than by choking it with cream. There are more ways than one of getting something done.

catch

Catch as catch can. Get all you can in the ways you know best.

chain

The chain is no stronger than its weakest link. If one part of the chain breaks, then the whole chain is completely useless.

change

There is nothing permanent except change. The only unchanging aspect of life is change.

A change is as good as a rest. A change of scene is often as effective as a holiday.

charity

Charity begins at home. The meaning of this has changed. It once meant that although charity began at home, it did not end there. Now it tends to mean 'you may need help, but I must help myself first'.

Charity covers a multitude of sins. Originally this read 'Charity shall cover the multitude of sins'. It means, you should be forgiving to those who sin.

chatters

Who chatters to you will chatter of you. If someone gossips freely to you, they will most likely gossip about you.

cheap

Ill ware is never cheap. A useless bargain will cost you more in the end.

cheat

He that will cheat at play will cheat you anyway. Anyone who cheats at a game will be a cheat in other ways.

Cheats never prosper. Deceit will not help you.

cheerful

A cheerful look makes a dish a feast. A happy face can turn something ordinary into something special.

chickens

Don't count your chickens before they're hatched. Don't assume you have gained something until it has been proved.

child

A burned child dreads the fire. A harsh experience is not easily forgotten.

9

SEEN BUT NOT HEARD

children
Little children should be seen and not heard. Children should be silent and not speak until they are spoken to.
Children and chicken must be always picking. Children are always hungry.

circumstances
Circumstances alter cases. If the conditions change, then the original agreement is no longer valid.

cleanliness
Cleanliness is next to godliness. A clean person is likely to be a moral person.

clothes
Clothes don't make the man. It is the person that matters, not the clothes they wear.

cloud
Every cloud has a silver lining. However unpleasant things are, something good will come out of them.

clouds
If there were no clouds, we should not enjoy the sun. If the sun shone all the time, you would not appreciate it.

coat
Cut your coat according to your cloth. Judge how much to spend by the amount you have available.

company
A man is known by the company he keeps. The world will judge you by those with whom you associate.

comparisons
Comparisons are odious. You should not make judgments between two people, since they will almost certainly be unjust.

contented
A contented mind is a perpetual feast. A contented mind gives lasting happiness.

cow
You can't sell the cow and drink the milk. You can't have it both ways: either you enjoy what you have or you sell it.

crab
You cannot make a crab walk straight. Don't attempt to do the impossible.

cradle
The hand that rocks the cradle rules the world. A mother's influence is one of the greatest of all.

credit
Give credit where credit is due. Praise should be given when it is deserved.

crown
Uneasy lies the head that wears a crown. Being a leader is not simple or safe.

crutches
One foot is better than two crutches. It is better to accept what you have, little though it be, than to risk something worse.

cry

Don't cry before you're hurt. Don't anticipate injury – it may not happen.

cup

There's many a slip 'twixt cup and lip. Until you actually have something in your possession, you can't be sure of it.

cured

What can't be cured must be endured. If nothing can be done to help the situation, then you must put up with it.

curiosity

Curiosity killed the cat. Being curious can lead you into trouble.

curses

Curses, like chickens, come home to roost. Those who threaten others may find they bring trouble upon themselves.

custom

Custom without reason is but ancient error. Because something has always been done, it should not be assumed that it is good practice.

D

darkest

The darkest hour is just before the dawn. Things may seem bad, but they will almost certainly improve.

dead

Dead men tell no tales. Once someone is dead they remain silent for ever.
He goes long barefoot that waits for a dead man's shoes. A warning about the folly of waiting for someone to die simply to gain their possessions.
Always speak well of the dead. Since they cannot answer for themselves, it is up to those remaining to speak well of them.

deaf

None is so deaf as those who won't hear. It is pointless trying to make someone listen who is determined not to.

death

Death is a great leveller. Death treats all people equally, no matter how important they were in life.

debt

Out of debt, out of danger. Owing money is worrying and settling a debt gives peace of mind.

deceives

If a man deceives me once, shame on him; if he deceives me twice, shame on me. If you have experienced deceit once, you would be foolish to allow it again.

He that once deceives is ever suspected. If you behave deceitfully, you will not be trusted again.

deeds

Deeds, not words. You are judged by what you do, rather than what you say.

despair

Despair gives courage to a coward. When there is no hope at all, even a coward has nothing to lose.

devil

Better the devil you know than the devil you don't. Something unknown is more frightening than something already experienced.

Every man for himself, and the devil take the hindmost. Look after yourself first and leave others to look after themselves.

He that sups with the devil must have a long spoon. If you having dealings with someone untrustworthy you must be very cautious.

The devil finds work for idle hands. Those who have nothing to do will end up by doing something wrong.

Give the devil his due. Assess someone fairly, even if they are not liked.

diamond

Diamond cut diamond. It takes someone of great strength to match another strong person.

die

Never say die. Never give up hope.

difficult

What is difficult is done at once; the impossible takes a little longer. Nothing is impossible.

dirt

Fling dirt enough and some will stick. If you tell enough unpleasant tales about someone, some of them will be believed.

Every man must eat a peck of dirt before he dies. No-one goes through life without some hurt or harm.

WHY KEEP A DOG AND BARK YOURSELF?

LOVE ME, LOVE MY DOG!

discretion
Discretion is the better part of valour. What appears to be cowardice may, in fact, be wise caution.

disease
The remedy may be worse than the disease. Don't be too hasty to correct what appears to be wrong. The remedy may cause more harm.

diseases
Desperate diseases call for desperate remedies. If you are in real trouble, a desperate decision might seem to be the only way out.

dish
No dish pleases all palates alike. Not everyone likes the same things.

distance
Distance lends enchantment to the view. Seen from a long way off, things may seem better than they really are.

do
Do as I say, not as I do. Never mind how I behave, do as I tell you.

Do as you would be done by. Behave to others as you would want them to treat you.

dog
Better to be the head of a dog than the tail of a lion. Better to be top of a small group than bottom of a large one.

Why keep a dog and bark yourself? If you have someone to do a job for you, there is no point in doing it yourself.

Dog does not eat dog. Those in crime do not give each other away.

Help a lame dog over a stile. Help someone in difficulties.

Love me, love my dog. Anyone who wants to be my friend must accept me as I am, with all my failings.

You can't teach an old dog new tricks. It's difficult for old people to learn new skills.

Give a dog a bad name and hang him. Once someone's reputation has been damaged they cannot retrieve it.

dogs
Two dogs strive for a bone and a third runs away with it. If you get into a dispute with someone, beware that a third person doesn't take advantage of your quarrel.

All are not thieves that dogs bark at. Don't judge by appearances.

door
A golden key opens every door. Money will give you an entrance anywhere.

If one door shuts, another opens. If you fail, try again; there will be other opportunities.

doubt
When in doubt, do nowt. When you're not sure, take no action.

ear

You can't make a silk purse out of a sow's ear. You can't make something of good quality from poor materials.

easy

Easy come, easy go. What was easily won is easily lost.

It's easy to be wise after the event. Once you know the outcome, it's a simple matter to suggest how things could have been done.

eggs

Don't teach your grandmother to suck eggs. Don't try to tell more experienced people how to do their jobs.

You can't make an omelette without breaking eggs. It's impossible to do anything without sacrificing something.

He that would have eggs must endure the cackling of hens. If you want something, you must be prepared to put up with some discomfort.

empty

Empty vessels make the most sound. Foolish people are also the noisiest.

end

All good things must come to an end. Nothing pleasant goes on for ever.

The end justifies the means. If the result is good, it doesn't matter what methods were used to achieve it.

envied

Better be envied than pitied. People who are envied are looked up to; those who are pitied are looked down upon.

err

To err is human. Everyone makes mistakes.

events

Coming events cast their shadows before. You usually get some idea of what is going to happen by clues in advance.

everything

Everything comes to him that waits. Someone who waits patiently will usually get what they want in the end.

A place for everything and everything in its place. Life is simpler and easier if you are tidy and methodical.

evils

Choose the lesser of two evils. If you have to choose between two bad choices, choose the least bad.

excuse

A bad excuse is better than none. This is said to those who offer a poor excuse.

expects

Blessed is he who expects nothing, for he shall never be disappointed. If you expect little from life, any pleasant surprise is a bonus.

experience

Experience is the mother of wisdom. As you learn, both by your mistakes and successes, you gain wisdom.

eye

The eye is bigger than the belly. This refers to someone who helps themselves to more food than they can really eat.

An eye for an eye, a tooth for a tooth. This refers to revenge, getting exact justice for crimes committed.

What the eye doesn't see, the heart doesn't grieve over. Things that happen without your knowledge, especially unpleasant ones, do not worry you.

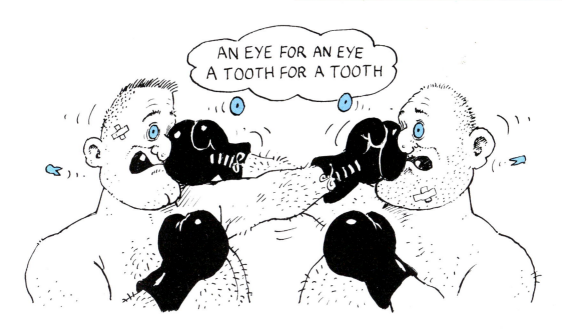

familiarity

Familiarity breeds contempt. The more familiar you are with a person or thing, the less respect you have.

father

Like father, like son. A child often behaves like its parents.
He whose father is judge, goes safe to his trial. Parents cannot judge their own children fairly.

feast

A contented mind is a perpetual feast. If you are contented, then you will enjoy peace of mind and happiness.

feathers

Fine feathers make fine birds. Said of people who dress well to impress others.

fiddle

There's many a good tune played on an old fiddle. Older people can be just as useful as young ones.

fight

He that fights and runs away may live to fight another day. Don't be foolhardy; save yourself for another battle.

finders

Finders keepers. Someone who finds something should be allowed to keep it.

first

First come, first served. The first to arrive will be the first to receive attention.

fish

That fish will soon be caught that nibbles at every bait. Curiosity and inquisitiveness will lead to your downfall.
The best fish swim near the bottom. The best things are the most difficult to obtain.
There are as good fish in the sea as ever came out of it. Things may have gone wrong this time, but another opportunity will come.

flatterer

When the flatterer pipes, then the devil dances. Flattery does not bring good, either to the flatterer or the person being flattered.

15

fool

Better to be a fool than a knave. Better to be innocent and foolish than guilty.
A fool and his money are soon parted. Don't be persuaded to spend money on things you don't really want or need.
There's no fool like an old fool. An elderly and experienced person can seem more foolish than a young one.

fools

Young men think old men fools, and old men know young men to be so. The enthusiasm of the young and the wisdom of the old never mix.

foot

Never tell your enemy that your foot aches. Don't expose your weaknesses to someone who can wield power over you.

THERE'S NO FOOL LIKE AN OLD FOOL

footprints

Footprints in the sands of time are not made by sitting down. People who have made their mark on the world have been active in what they do.

forbidden

Forbidden fruit is sweetest. Something that is forbidden always seems more desirable and exciting.

forelock

Take time by the forelock. Take advantage of the present, the past cannot be changed.

forewarned

Forewarned is forearmed. Knowing about future danger helps you to cope with it when it arrives.

forgive

Forgive and forget. Don't harbour feelings of revenge; put such thoughts from your mind.

fortune

Fortune favours the bold. People who act bravely deserve, and find, good luck.
Fortune knocks at least once at every man's gate. When an opportunity comes, seize it.

friend

A friend in need is a friend indeed. Someone who helps you when you are in trouble is a true friend.

friends

The best of friends must part. However pleasant, all relationships must come to an end.
May God defend me from my friends; I can defend myself from my enemies. A misguided friend can do far more damage than an enemy.

IT'S BETTER TO GIVE THAN TO RECEIVE

gate
A creaking gate hangs long. Those who are not in good health often last longest.

give
It's better to give than receive. It's better to be generous than to take from others.

gluttony
Gluttony kills more than the sword. Overeating is dangerous and can kill.

gnats
Men strain at gnats and swallow camels. Some people concern themselves with small wrongs and overlook large ones.

God
God helps those who help themselves. Don't expect to get something without working for it first.
You cannot serve God and mammon. You must choose between holy and worldly things.
All things are possible with God. With God's help you can do anything.

gods
The mills of the gods grind slowly, but they grind exceedingly small. Rewards and punishments may not come immediately, but they will come in the end.

gold
All that glitters is not gold. What looks attractive at first may prove to be worthless.
When we have gold we are in fear, when we have none we are in danger. If someone is rich, they are afraid of thieves; if someone is poor they have no means of support.

goose
Don't kill the goose that lays the golden eggs. Don't cut off the source of your success or profit.
What's sauce for the goose is sauce for the gander. What's good for one person is good for another; you can't complain if you are treated equally.
He that has a goose will get a goose. The rich continue to get richer.

grasp
Grasp all, lose all. Don't be greedy, or you may lose what you already have.

17

grass

The grass is always greener on the other side of the fence. Discontent with what you have leads you to believe that others are more fortunate.

Greek

When Greek meets Greek, then comes the tug of war. When two equally-matched opponents meet, it becomes a real struggle.

ground

He that lies upon the ground can fall no lower. One compensation for being at the bottom of the ladder is that you can't fall any lower.

growing

A growing youth has a wolf in his belly. The young are always hungry.

guest

A constant guest is never welcome. A too-frequent visitor can earn the dislike of his or her friends.

hands

Many hands make light work. If the task is shared by many, then it will be easier.

handsome

Handsome is as handsome does. The character of a person should be decided by their actions, not by their appearance.

hare

First catch your hare. Wait till you've got what you need before you decide what to do with it.

You can't run with the hare and hunt with the hounds. You can't be friendly with two opposing types of people.

hares

If you run after two hares, you'll catch neither. Don't do two things at once.

haste

Make haste slowly. Think carefully before you rush into something; give it time and thought.

Haste trips over its own heels or *More haste, less speed.* When you try to do something in a hurry it often takes longer due to carelessness.

hasty

A hasty man drinks his tea with a fork. Another version of the 'haste' proverbs.

hay

Make hay while the sun shines. Take advantage of something while it is available.

MANY HANDS MAKE LIGHT WORK

head

You can't put an old head on young shoulders. You can't expect a young person to have the judgment of someone older and more experienced.

heads

Two heads are better than one. In a difficulty it's better to seek advice rather than carrying on alone.

health

Health is better than wealth. It's better to be healthy than rich.

heart

It's a sad heart that never rejoices. No-one should be sad or miserable all the time.

hearts

Kind hearts are more than coronets. It's your character that matters, not your social standing.

heat

If you don't like the heat, get out of the kitchen. If the pace is too fast for you, then step aside and allow others more capable to take over.

hedge

A hedge between keeps friendship green. or *Love your neighbour, yet pull not down your hedge*. People are likely to be better friends when they don't see too much of each other.

heels

One pair of heels is often worth two pairs of hands. When the odds are against you, it's better to run than to stand and fight.

hell

The road to hell is paved with good intentions. Good intentions aren't enough; deeds are what count.

help

A little help is worth a deal of pity. It's better to give real help to someone rather than offer them sympathy.

hesitates

He who hesitates is lost. Anyone who delays will lose their chance of success.

history

History repeats itself. If it has happened once, it will happen again.

hog

What can you expect from a hog but a grunt? If an ill-mannered person is rude to you, it's only what you should expect.

home

East or west, home's best, or *There's no place like home*. Home is the best place to be.

honesty

Honesty is the best policy. You will always gain the trust of people by being honest.

hook

The bait hides the hook. An attractive bargain may have a hidden flaw.

hope

If it were not for hope, the heart would break. Everyone needs hope to recover from their troubles and griefs.

Hope for the best, but prepare for the worst. Optimism is fine, but always be cautious.

Hope springs eternal in the human breast. People are always hoping.

horse

It's useless flogging a dead horse. It's no use trying to get satisfaction from something which cannot provide it.

You can lead a horse to water, but you can't make him drink. You can't force someone to do something they don't want to do.

Don't look a gift horse in the mouth. Don't criticize something which has been freely given to you.

All lay loads on a willing horse. Anyone who is willing and good-natured is likely to be asked to do more than others.

Every horse thinks its own pack is heaviest. Everyone believes that they are doing the most work.

houses

People who live in glass houses shouldn't throw stones. People with faults of their own should not complain of faults in others.

hunger

Hunger is the best sauce. If you're really hungry, you need no sauce to give you an appetite.

ignorance

Where ignorance is bliss, 'tis folly to be wise. If you are happy not knowing something, then it is better that way.

imitation

Imitation is the sincerest form of flattery. If you copy someone's ideas or ways, then you obviously admire that person.

impressions

First impressions are the most rewarding. The feelings you have about someone at the first meeting are likely to stay with you.

inspiration

Ninety per cent of inspiration is perspiration. Most good ideas don't come easily, but from hard work.

Jack

A Jack of all trades is master of none. Someone who tries their hand at too many things will never be expert in any.

jam

Jam tomorrow and jam yesterday; but never jam today. People remember the good things of yesterday and look forward to the future, but never appreciate the good things of the moment.

jest

There's many a true word spoken in jest. Even though a remark is made as a joke, it often contains an element of truth.

joy

Sudden joy kills sooner than excessive grief. Sudden great excitement is more likely to kill than long grief.

just

A just war is better than an unjust peace. It is better to fight for a fair world than live in an unfair one.

kindness

Kindness comes of will. Kindness cannot be obtained by force.

knowledge

Doubt is the key of knowledge. Curiosity will lead you to learn more.

labourer

The labourer is worthy of his hire. Anyone who does an honest job deserves to be paid adequately.

ladder

He who would climb the ladder must begin at the bottom. Whoever starts at the bottom will learn all there is to know as they rise to the top.

late

Better late than never. It's better to arrive late than not at all.

laugh

Laugh and the world laughs with you; weep and you weep alone. Everyone wants to share the joy of a cheerful person, but they shun someone who is miserable.

lazy

Lazy people take the most pains. Those who take short cuts in their work will have to do it again, and so end up doing more work.

leap

Look before you leap. Think carefully before you act.

learn

Never too old to learn. No-one is so old that they can't usefully learn new things.

A LEOPARD, TRYING TO CHANGE ITS SPOTS

learning

A little learning is a dangerous thing. Those who know only a little can deceive themselves into believing they know all.

leisure

Idle people have the least leisure. If you are idle all the time you cannot know the pleasure of leisure.

lend

Lend and lose the loan, or gain an enemy. If you lend something you must expect to lose it, or to offend by asking for it back.

leopard

The leopard can't change its spots. People's characters remain the same, no matter how much else changes.

liar

A liar is not believed when he tells the truth. If you lie, people will assume that everything you say is untrue.

liars

Liars should have good memories. Liars frequently forget what they have lied about, and so give themselves away by telling a different lie.

liberty

Lean liberty is better than fat slavery. It is better to be free and without riches than rich and enslaved.

lie

One lie makes many. If you tell one lie, you'll often have to tell many more to support it.

life

Where there's life, there's hope. As long as you are alive there is always something to look forward to.
Life is short and time is swift. Make the most of life.

lightning

Lightning never strikes twice in the same place. The same unusual happenings and events do not occur more than once to the same person.

listeners

Listeners never hear any good of themselves. If you eavesdrop on a conversation, the chances are you'll hear criticism of yourself.

live

Live not to eat, but eat to live. Gluttony is not to be recommended, you should eat only as much as is necessary for life.

love

The course of true love never did run smooth. Those in love will encounter problems on the way.
All's fair in love and war. When strong emotions are involved, you cannot have any real rules.

It is love that makes the world go round.

It is love that makes the world go round. Love is so necessary to people that it seems to move the Earth and the Sun. *Love is blind.* Those in love cannot see faults in their partners.

lucky

It's better to be born lucky than rich. If you're rich you only have money; if you're lucky you may have other gifts which money can't buy.

lump

If you don't like it, you can lump it. Whether you like it or not, you have to put up with it.

M

marry

Marry in haste and repent at leisure. If two people marry without due consideration, it is likely to be unsuccessful.

masters

No man can serve two masters. You can't be totally loyal to two people or two ideas at the same time.

meat

One man's meat is another man's poison. The fact that one person enjoys something doesn't mean that everyone else will.

mend

It's never too late to mend. It's never too late to change your ways for the better.

minds

Little things please little minds. People of small intellect are happy doing simple things.
Great minds think alike. Wise people tend to come to the same conclusions.

GREAT MINDS THINK ALIKE

misfortunes

Misfortunes never come singly. One mishap is often followed by another.

Our worst misfortunes are those which never happen. The calamities that we worry about most are the ones that tend not to happen.

miss

A miss is as good as a mile. If you fail in a small way, you might just as well have failed in a big way.

mistakes

He who makes no mistakes makes nothing. If you are so careful that you never make a mistake, you aren't likely to achieve very much.

Wise men learn by other men's mistakes; fools by their own. If you observe the mistakes of others you are unlikely to repeat them yourself.

money

The love of money is the root of all evil. Almost all of the world's evils are caused by greed.

Lend your money and lose a friend. Friendships are broken when you ask for a debt to be repaid.

Money is a good servant, but a bad master. Don't let money be your god, but use it well.

mountain

If the mountain will not come to Muhammad, Muhammad must go to the mountain. If whatever is needed cannot or will not come to a person, then that person must go and find it for themselves.

mouse

Don't make yourself a mouse, or the cat will eat you. Don't make yourself look small, or bullies will take advantage of you.

mouths

Out of the mouths of babes and sucklings. Wise remarks coming from the very young.

name

A good name is sooner lost than won. It takes time to earn a good name. If it is lost, it is lost for ever.

A man lives a generation; a name to the end of all generations. A family name does not die out but is passed on through the generations.

naughty

Naughty boys sometimes make good men. Those who were badly behaved in their youth often become well-respected in their adulthood.

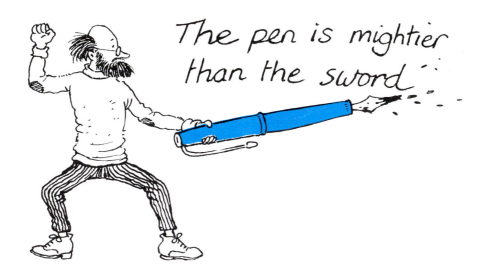

The pen is mightier than the sword

necessity

Necessity is the mother of invention.
When you are faced with a difficult
problem, you will often think of an
ingenious way out.

news

Bad news travels fast. Bad news reaches
you more quickly than good news.
No news is good news. News can be
good or bad; the fact that there is no
news means that all could be well.

nothing

Nothing venture, nothing gain. If you try
nothing, you will gain nothing.

numbers

There's safety in numbers. If many other
people are doing or thinking as you do,
then you are probably safer.

oaks

Many strokes fell tall oaks. A big task
can be completed by long and patient
work.

obey

He that cannot obey, cannot command.
If you are unable to obey orders, then
you're unlikely to be able to give them
yourself.

one

*One thing at a time, and that done well,
is a very good thing, as many can tell.*
Don't try to do too many things at
once, but do one task well.

pains

No pains, no gains. You won't gain
anything without some trouble.

parsnips

Fine words butter no parsnips. Fine talk
is all very well, but it doesn't produce
results.

pen

The pen is mightier than the sword.
What is written can often have more
power than brute force.

pence
Take care of the pence and the pounds will look after themselves. If you take care of the small details, the rest will fall into place.

penny
In for a penny, in for a pound. If you have decided to take part in something, you might just as well do it wholeheartedly.
A penny for your thoughts? What are you thinking about?

pin
He that will not stoop for a pin shall never be worth a pound. If you don't consider small profits, you will never be rich.

pint
You can't get a pint into a quart pot. You can't do the impossible.

piper
He who pays the piper calls the tune. If you are paying for something you are entitled to say how it is to be done.

pot
A watched pot never boils. Worrying about a situation will not help.

praise
Praise makes good men better and bad men worse. Good people are able to accept praise, but bad ones allow it to go to their heads.

present
There's no time like the present. If something needs to be done, then it should be done now.

prevention
Prevention is better than cure. It's always better to stop something from happening rather than to put it right after it has taken place.

price
Every man has his price. Anyone can be persuaded to do something by the offer of a bribe.

pride
Pride goes before a fall. A proud person is likely to fall into trouble.

procrastination
Procrastination is the thief of time. Do what needs to be done quickly; to delay simply wastes time.

purse
He that has a full purse never needed a friend. The well-off are rarely short of friends.
A heavy purse makes a light heart. Those with enough money can afford to be happy.

quarrel
It takes two to make a quarrel. There are two sides to every argument.

questions
Ask no questions and you'll be told no lies. Said to those who persist in asking awkward questions.

race
Slow but sure wins the race. Those who hurry may stumble; those who take care will win.

rains
It never rains but it pours. When disaster comes, it comes in plenty.

rats

Rats desert a sinking ship. Disloyal and untrustworthy people are the first to disappear if you are in trouble.

receiver

The receiver is as bad as the thief. Whoever deals in stolen goods is as guilty as the thief himself.

rod

Spare the rod and spoil the child. If punishment is not meted out to a bad child, he or she will suffer in the long run.

rose

A rose by any other name would smell as sweet. It doesn't matter what something is called; it's the thing itself that is important.
No rose without a thorn. Nothing is ever perfect.

rosebuds

Gather ye rosebuds while ye may. Take what pleasures you can now; you may not be able to do so later.

roundabouts

What you lose on the swings you gain on the roundabouts. What you lose on one thing, you gain on another.

S

sands

The sands of time are running out. There is not much time left.

scholars

The greatest scholars are not always the wisest men. Being learned doesn't make you wise in all things.

seeing

Seeing is believing. You have to accept the evidence of your own eyes.

self

Self-preservation is the first law of nature. Look after yourself first.

seven

Rain before seven, fine before eleven. A weather proverb: early showers often clear to give a fine day.

shadow

Catch not the shadow and lose the substance. Don't get so involved with the detail of something that you miss the main point.

SLOW BUT SURE WINS THE RACE

sheep

There's a black sheep in every flock. Every family (or group of people) has its rogue.

You might as well be hanged for a sheep as a lamb. If you are going to do something wrong, you might just as well commit a greater crime as a smaller one.

ship

It's no use spoiling the ship for a ha'porth of tar. If a job's worth doing, it's worth doing well.

sight

Out of sight, out of mind. If something is not seen, it is soon forgotten.

silence

Speech is silver, silence is golden. Sometimes it is better and more eloquent to remain silent.

sins

The sins of the fathers are visited upon the children. People are punished for the misdeeds of their forebears.

sky

A red sky at night is the shepherd's delight. A red sky in the morning is the shepherd's warning. A weather proverb, warning of fine weather, or rain.

sow

As you sow, so shall you reap. Your eventual reward will be based on how you lived your life.

speak

Speak well of your friend, of your enemy say nothing. If you can't say something good, say nothing.

speaks

He that speaks well, fights well. The person who is honest can be trusted to fight alongside you.

spirit

The spirit is willing, but the flesh is weak. However much you wish to do something, you may find yourself incapable of doing it.

sprat

To throw out a sprat to catch a mackerel. To sacrifice something of small importance in order to achieve something much bigger.

spur

Never spur a willing horse. Don't try to make a willing person do more than they can. They may end up by doing less.

step

Step after step the ladder is ascended. Persevere and, sooner or later, you will achieve your aim.

sticks

Sticks and stones may break my bones, but words will never hurt me. Jeering at me won't do any harm.

stitch

A stitch in time saves nine. Take action now, and save a greater problem later.

WHO RIDES A TIGER IS AFRAID TO DISMOUNT.

stone

Cast not the first stone. Before you criticize others, make sure you are not guilty yourself.

A rolling stone gathers no moss. Someone who frequently moves from place to place will not pick up habits and ways, good or bad.

straw

The last straw breaks the camel's back. This is said when a point is reached beyond which patience and endurance cannot go.

A drowning man will clutch at a straw. When all else has failed, people in a desperate situation will turn to anything which offers the slightest hope.

sublime

From the sublime to the ridiculous is but a step. Sometimes it doesn't require a large change to move from a serious situation to a laughable one.

success

Nothing succeeds like success. Once you succeed, you gain confidence to move on to even greater successes.

sundial

What's the good of a sundial in the shade? If you have talent, then don't hide it from the world.

sure

Better to be sure than sorry. It's better to choose a safe path than take a dangerous one unnecessarily.

swallow

One swallow doesn't make a summer. Because something pleasant has taken place doesn't mean that things in general have improved.

sweep

If each would sweep before his own door, we should have a clean city. If every individual did something to help, then life would be better for everyone.

tale

A good tale is none the worse for being told twice. People are prepared to hear an interesting story more than once.

thorn

I'll not pull the thorn out of your foot and put it in my own. I will help you, but not if it injures me.

tiger

Who rides a tiger is afraid to dismount. If you're doing something wrong, it's hard to stop, in case you are found out.

29

time

Time is the great healer. Grief and misery will heal in time.

Time and tide wait for no man. If you have something important to do, see that it is done immediately.

An inch of gold will not buy an inch of time. Nothing can buy back wasted time.

For the busy man time passes quickly. Time doesn't hang heavy for those with plenty to do.

tomorrow

Never put off till tomorrow what may be done today. If something needs to be done, don't delay by putting it off until another day.

Here today and gone tomorrow. Some things last for only a short time.

tongue

A still tongue makes a wise head. If you talk too much, you are liable to miss words of wisdom from others.

tooth

The tongue ever turns to the aching tooth. When something worries you, you are likely to keep thinking about it.

tortoise

The tortoise wins the race while the hare is sleeping. From one of *Aesop's Fables*. Slow and sure will win in the end.

travel

It is better to travel hopefully than to arrive. If you are working towards a goal, the work itself is often more rewarding than the completion.

trouble

Don't meet trouble half-way. Don't worry about something before it actually happens.

A trouble shared is a trouble halved. If you confide in someone about misfortune, it is easier to bear.

trust

Put your trust in God, but keep your powder dry. Trust in God, but nevertheless take every precaution yourself.

truth

Speak the truth and shame the devil. However much you are tempted to lie, it is always better to speak the truth.

Truth is stranger than fiction. Things in real life can often be much odder than something invented.

turn

One good turn deserves another. If someone helps you, try to help them in return.

unexpected

Nothing is so certain as the unexpected. It is certain that things which are unexpected will surprise you.

united

United we stand, divided we fall. If people work together, they have a stronger chance of winning through.

variety

Variety is the spice of life. People get bored with the same old things; something new arouses their interest.

virtue

Virtue is its own reward. You should never expect to be rewarded for a good deed. The satisfaction you get from doing it should be enough.

volunteer

One volunteer is worth two pressed men. Those who are compelled to do something are much less likely to do the job well than someone who is willing.

wagon

Hitch your wagon to a star. Always aim high.
When the wagon of fortune goes well, spite and envy hang onto the wheels. Good luck will always cause jealousy in others.

walk

Learn to walk before you run. Take things in easy stages, and learn as you go along.

walls

Walls have ears. Don't speak too freely; you may be overheard.
Men, not walls, make a city safe. Wise government, not armed might, is the best protection of a country.

waste

Waste not, want not. If you're careful with what you have, you'll not go hungry.

waters

Still waters run deep. Quiet people are often the deepest thinkers.

way

Better to ask the way than go astray. If you are unsure about something, it is better to take advice.

wear

It's better to wear out than rust out. It's better to be active than idle.

wheel

The worst wheel on the cart creaks most. The most inefficient person is the one who makes most complaints.

will

Where there's a will, there's a way. If you are determined to do something, you will find a way of doing it.
Will is no skill. Wanting to do something is not the same as being able to do it.

wind

It's an ill wind that blows nobody any good. Somebody, somewhere is able to profit from misfortune.

wish

The wish is father to the thought. If you wish something were true, you can sometimes believe that it really is so.

wishes

If wishes were horses, beggars would ride. If all we needed was to wish for something, then we could all be rich.

wolf

When the wolf comes in at the door, love flies out of the window. If people fall on hard times even love finds it difficult to survive.

words

A man of words and not of deeds is like a garden full of weeds. This describes someone who talks all the time rather than taking action.

worm

Even a worm will turn. Even the mildest of people will react if pushed too far.

worse

Worse things happen at sea. It could have been worse!

wound

Though the wound be healed, yet a scar remains. People do not forget the pain of old hurts and the lesson learned from them.

wrath

Let not the sun go down on your wrath. If you have an argument or quarrel, make every effort to settle it amicably before the day ends.

wrong

If anything can go wrong, it will. Even the best-laid plans can go awry.

wrongs

Two wrongs don't make a right. If someone does you a wrong, then having your revenge will not make things right.

yesterday

It's too late to call back yesterday. What has passed is gone and cannot be recaptured.

young

You're only young once. Take advantage of your youth while you have it.

yourself

Yourself first, others afterwards. Put your own self-interests before the good of others.

youth

Youth and age will not agree. The younger generation will never agree with the older one.

I AM THE WORM WHO TURNED!